Very G

D0458254

# Lee Bailey's

**CORN**

*by Lee Bailey*

*Photographs by Tom Eckerle*

CLARKSON POTTER/PUBLISHERS
NEW YORK

Published by Clarkson Potter/Publishers, 201 East 50th Street, New York, New York 10022. Member of the Crown Publishing Group.

Random House, Inc. New York, Toronto, London, Sydney, Auckland

CLARKSON N. POTTER, POTTER and colophon are trademarks of Clarkson N. Potter, Inc.

Manufactured in Japan
Design by Howard Klein
Library of Congress Cataloging-in-Publication Data

Bailey, Lee.
    [Corn]
    Lee Bailey's corn / by Lee Bailey : photographs by Tom Eckerle.
        p.   cm.
    1. Cookery (Corn)   I. Title.
    TX809.M2B35   1993
    641.6'567—dc20                                      92-30642
                                                             CIP

ISBN 0-517-59236-3
10 9 8 7 6 5 4 3 2 1
First Edition

As always, my thanks to all the people at Clarkson Potter, and to Tom Eckerle for his beautiful photography. Thanks to Lee Klein for supervision and to Libby for her help.

Very special thanks to Townie Krawcheck, Terrell Vermont, and John Taylor, who made work a pleasure.

And to Judy and Fred Reinhard, thanks for allowing us to use things from their lovely shop called fred. Finally, my appreciation to Trey Wilson for his barbecued corn recipe.

I'd hazard a guess that, along with vine-ripened tomatoes, just-picked corn steamed on the cob must be on the top of everyone's Favorite Summer Vegetables list. O.K. O.K. I know tomatoes are technically fruit, but what you have here is poetic license.

Whatever, corn seems to make us all behave like kids with butter on our noses. Remember being told to calm down because you and your cousins had got too rambunctious, vying to see who could chomp down and back a row of corn kernels the fastest? Obviously this didn't have too much to do with gracious dining. This was corn as sport. Corn for sporty dining is something else again.

Here's another thing I've noticed. Maybe it's just coincidence, but I have three friends who don't hardly know how to boil water (you know who you are)—all women—who are absolutely bananas about corn. That, of course, is not unusual since most anyone in his right mind is slightly crazed about the stuff. The distinction here is that this trio of nevercooks almost demands that you allow them to prepare the corn when one of them is visiting for the weekend. This can be an experience, if you know what I mean. For one thing, everyone must follow strict orders when *she* is at the helm in the kitchen: "Now sit down—it'll be out in a minute—get the butter ready—is everyone at the table? . . . Come on, eat it while it's hot. It won't be any good if it gets cold. I'll put another batch in the steamer just as you are finishing the first cob. . . . What's that burning—did I leave the steamer on the heat?" Of course, this would be a pain in the neck under other circumstances, but their corn always tastes terrific, and, oddly, the ritual does seem to enhance the occasion. Sure, you wouldn't want to do it that way every time—but for a change of pace.

Anyway, what I'm asking is, why do people who don't know how to cook like to cook corn? Is this some sort of fluke, or more corn as sport?

All right, enough foolishness. On to the recipes. There's lots here. For instance, I've given you ways to serve corn as a first course, besides on the cob. Try it with ham in fritters, in timbales, or souffléed, for example, each topped by one of the sauces you'll find at the end of the book. Or toss kernels with prosciutto.

Corn folded into an omelet and accompanied by salad is great as the main attraction for a lunch. Ditto for savory corn pie with a delicious cheddar crust (small portions of this could do double duty as a first course). And while we are on the subject of lunch, how about a marinated shrimp and corn combination—pretty tasty stuff if I do say so myself—or corn-stuffed peppers.

If you are casting about for a main course, consider corn and fresh salmon croquettes with your favorite homemade tartar sauce. Or there is a corn and gorgonzola sauce piqued with lemon rind, fresh mint, and basil to top fettuccine. As an accompaniment to the main course, corn can fill many slots—muffins, pudding, spoon bread, or simply creamed. You shouldn't overlook corn relish, which was always a great favorite with cold meats in our house when I was growing up.

For the kids, popcorn balls! And for breakfast, sweet corn cakes just aching to be served with maple syrup, preserves, and homemade sausage patties.

But wait, there's one last surprise—a corn dessert. And I don't mean some version of Indian pudding, the message from which I never got anyway. It's a corn and coconut ice cream from Thailand. You'll love it.

Happy corn season.

# Recipes

---

# CORN KERNEL MUFFINS

———◆———

You might add caraway seeds to these.

> *2 cups white cornmeal*
> *½ cup flour*
> *3½ teaspoons baking powder*
> *½ teaspoon baking soda*
> *1½ teaspoons salt*
> *1½ cups buttermilk*
> *2 eggs, lightly beaten*
> *2 tablespoons unsalted butter, melted*
> *3 to 4 cups fresh corn kernels (scrape the cobs)*

Preheat the oven to 450 degrees. Grease two 12-cup muffin tins and set aside.

Sift together the cornmeal, flour, baking powder, baking soda, and salt. Lightly stir in the buttermilk and then the eggs. Do not overmix. Add butter and corn. Stir just enough to blend. Fill prepared cups and bake for 25 minutes.

*Makes 18 to 24 muffins depending on size of tins*

# CORN KERNEL CORN BREAD

◆

The poblano chili peppers called for here are not so hot as jalapeños. Canned chili peppers may be substituted.

You can make this either of two ways, depending on how much crust you like. By reducing the buttermilk to just enough to hold the batter together—say, between ¼ and ½ cup—you will get a rather flat corn bread that is almost all crunch. (You may have to pat the stiff batter into the pan.)

*1 cup yellow cornmeal*
*1 cup flour*
*1 teaspoon sugar*
*1¼ teaspoons salt*
*3¾ teaspoons baking powder*
*¼ teaspoon baking soda*
*2 cups fresh corn kernels*
*¼ cup seeded and minced poblano chilis*
*1 cup plus 2 tablespoons buttermilk*
*¼ cup vegetable oil, plus additional*
*1 egg, lightly beaten*

Preheat the oven to 400 degrees and place a 10-inch cast-iron skillet in the oven to preheat too.

Sift the dry ingredients together into a large bowl. Toss in the corn and chili peppers. Combine the liquid ingredients in another bowl and then stir lightly into the dry. Do not overmix. Quickly remove heated skillet from the oven and coat with vegetable oil. Pour the batter in and bake until golden, about 40 minutes. The reduced buttermilk version will take a bit longer.

*Serves 8 or more*

# CORN KERNEL SPOON BREAD

———◆———

Spoon bread suits me almost any time, but with fresh corn it's even better.

> **1¼ cups milk**
> **¾ cup white cornmeal**
> **¾ teaspoon salt**
> **2 tablespoons butter**
> **1 17-ounce can yellow creamed corn**
> **¾ teaspoon baking powder**
> **3 egg yolks, beaten until thick**
> **3 egg whites, beaten into stiff peaks**

Preheat the oven to 375 degrees. Grease a 2-quart baking dish.

Heat the milk in a saucepan over low heat until bubbles form around the edge. Stir in the cornmeal and salt, and continue to cook over low heat, stirring constantly, until the mixture thickens, about 10 minutes. Stir in the butter and corn, then the baking powder. Stir in the yolks and fold in the whites. Pour into the prepared dish and bake until puffy and golden, about 35 minutes.

*Serves 6*

# CORN SOUFFLE

———◆———

Corn Soufflé, dressed up with one of the sauces you'll find on pages 76–79, could be the centerpiece of a casual lunch or a first course.

*2 tablespoons unsalted butter*
*2 tablespoons flour*
*1 cup milk*
*3 medium eggs, separated*
*2 generous cups fresh corn kernels (scrape the cobs)*
*1 teaspoon sugar*
*1 teaspoon salt*
*¼ teaspoon white pepper*

Preheat the oven to 350 degrees. Generously grease a 6-cup soufflé dish. Put a kettle of water on to heat over low heat.

Melt the butter in a medium saucepan over medium heat and sprinkle flour over, stirring and cooking for a few minutes until well blended. Whisk in milk and continue to cook, whisking until mixture is thickened, about 3 minutes. Beat yolks with a fork and add a little of the white sauce to warm them. Pour the yolks back into the sauce, whisking. Cook for another minute. Off the heat, whisk in all other ingredients except egg whites. Allow to cool slightly. Beat egg whites into soft peaks and fold into the corn mixture. Pour into soufflé dish and bake in a water bath until puffy and browned, about 35 minutes.

*Serves 6*

# CORN OMELET

——◆——

You should use tender white corn just cut from the cob when you make this.

Making an omelet is simple and quick after you get the technique down—as those who've made them know. If omelet making is new to you, give it a try with your breakfast eggs mixed with a little water, salt, and pepper. Some people also add about a tablespoon of chopped chilled butter to the mixture just before adding it to the pan. You'll get the hang of it quickly.

> *2 or 3 eggs*
> *1½ teaspoons water*
> *½ cup fresh white corn kernels (scrape the cobs)*
> *2 teaspoons snipped chives*
> *Salt and black pepper*
> *1½ teaspoons unsalted butter*

Beat the eggs and water together lightly. Stir in the corn, chives, salt, and pepper. Heat an omelet pan or a small skillet with curved sides. Melt the butter in the pan over medium heat, tilting it as you do so the entire surface is coated.

When the butter stops bubbling and is just beginning to turn brown, pour in the egg mixture. Stir a few seconds with the tines of a fork, without scraping the bottom. Lifting the pan slightly off the heat and shaking, lift the edges of the congealing egg to allow as much of the egg as possible to run under. At the same time start tilting the pan slightly and begin inching one side of the cooked omelet to fold it over. When it is almost folded, tilt the pan enough to make the omelet roll onto the far side of the pan. Allow to cook a few seconds more before inverting onto a warmed plate.

*Makes 1 omelet*

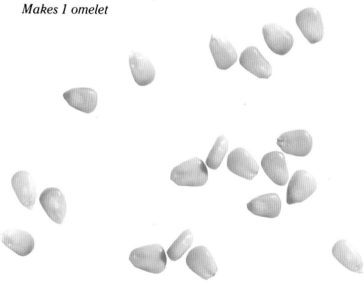

OVERLEAF: *Corn Omelet.*

# CORN PUDDING

———◆———

Corn pudding has always been a popular dish in my native South. The recipe here is one my family used to serve all the time. You might want to use an egg substitute here.

*2½ cups fresh corn kernels (scrape the cobs)*
*1 cup light cream*
*1 tablespoon sugar*
*1½ teaspoons salt*
*¼ teaspoon white pepper*
*3 tablespoons unsalted butter, melted*
*5 eggs, well beaten*
*3 cups milk*
*1 tablespoon cornstarch*
*1 tablespoon cold water*

Preheat the oven to 350 degrees. Generously grease a shallow 2-quart baking dish.

Place the corn and cream in the top of a double boiler and cook for 10 to 20 minutes, stirring often to prevent sticking, to reduce slightly. This should produce a thickened creamy mixture. If it starts to dry out, add a little more cream and if it is too liquid, cook a little longer.

Measure the mixture. If you don't have 2½ cups, add a little extra cream to make up the difference. Set aside to cool for about 15 minutes.

Combine the corn mixture with all other ingredients except the cornstarch and water. Mix the cornstarch with the cold water to make a paste and stir into other ingredients. Pour into the baking dish and cook until set and firm, about 1 hour.

*Serves 6 to 8*

# CORN TIMBALES

———◆———

Another one of those old Southern favorites. Tasty and simple.

*¼ cup heavy cream*
*½ cup chicken stock*
*2 cups fresh corn kernels*
*¼ teaspoon black pepper*

Preheat the oven to 350 degrees. Grease eight ½-cup ramekins.

Combine the ingredients, reserving 1 cup of the kernels. Place mixture in a food processor and process until smooth. Stir in the reserved kernels and divide between the ramekins. Bake in a hot water bath for 25 minutes, or until set. Allow to rest a few minutes before loosening edges and unmolding.

You might garnish these with roasted red bell peppers— chopped or cut into strips.

*Serves 8*

# FRIED CORN

We had this during my childhood, but it was made with "horse corn"—that is, corn with big sturdy yellow kernels, not the tender sweet white or white and yellow corn so popular today. This sturdiness made it possible to brown the kernels more than you can with the softer varieties, giving it a very nutty flavor.

> *2 tablespoons canola oil*
> *1 tablespoon unsalted butter*
> *1 tablespoon bacon fat*
> *10 ears of corn, kernels cut and scraped from*
> *cobs*

Heat the oil, butter, and bacon fat in a large skillet over medium-high heat until very hot. Add the corn quickly, stirring to coat. Continue to stir as the corn cooks, later scraping up any that stick to the bottom. Sample after a few minutes for doneness. The cooking time will depend on the age and kind of corn. Add salt if desired.

*Serves 6 to 8*

# CREAMED CORN

This is a good way to use older large-kernel corn.

> **4 cups fresh corn kernels (scrape the cobs)**
> **2 cups milk or light cream**
> **1¼ cups warm water**
> **1 teaspoon sugar**
> **¼ teaspoon salt**
> **2 teaspoons unsalted butter (optional)**

Put the corn and milk in a small saucepan and bring to a boil. Reduce heat and simmer, stirring with a fork every once in a while, until milk is almost completely reduced, about 15 minutes. Add the water and cook another 10 minutes, until liquid has reduced to just below the surface of the corn. Remove from the heat and stir in the sugar and salt. Process ¾ cup of the kernels in a food processor, then stir the puree back in with the kernels. Add the butter if desired.

*Serves 6*

# SKILLET CORN

———◆———

Everyone loves this easy-to-prepare concoction. The trick is to have the iron skillet in which it is cooked super-hot when the corn mixture goes in.

> *2 tablespoons vegetable oil*
> *8 medium ears of white corn, kernels cut and*
>     *scraped from the cobs*
> *½ teaspoon salt*
> *½ cup flour*

Place an 8-inch cast-iron skillet in a 425 degree oven. After about 20 minutes, pour the vegetable oil into the skillet.

Meanwhile, combine all the other ingredients to make a thick batter.

Remove the skillet from the oven and pour (and scrape) the batter in. Do not stir; press the batter into place, and be careful not to burn yourself.

Bake until a nice crust forms on the bottom and the top starts to brown. Remove and invert onto a serving plate. Cut into 4 wedges. This will be rather crumbly, so use a spatula and a fork to serve.

*Serves 4*

OVERLEAF: *Skillet Corn.*

# WARM CORN AND PROSCIUTTO

———◆———

This makes a quick and easy first course. For best results use
*very* fresh corn.

> **2 tablespoons unsalted butter**
> **8 to 10 ears of corn, kernels cut and scraped**
> **from the cobs**
> **1 to 2 tablespoons milk, half-and-half, or light**
> **cream**
> **Salt to taste**
> **1 teaspoon sugar**
> **3 ounces thinly sliced prosciutto, cut into thin**
> **strips**

Heat the butter in a large skillet over medium heat. When
bubbling, toss in the corn kernels. Add the milk and cook over
very low heat for several minutes, until just barely tender. The
timing will depend on the variety and age of the corn used.
Season with salt and sugar, then toss in the prosciutto.

*Serves 6*

# PASTA WITH GORGONZOLA AND
# WHITE CORN SAUCE

———◆———

The thing to remember here is not to allow this sauce to boil after the cheese is stirred in or when it is reheated—it will become bitter. It should be hot, of course.

*6 tablespoons minced red onion*
*¼ cup olive oil*
*¼ teaspoon salt (or to taste)*
*1½ cups evaporated skim milk*
*6 ounces sweet gorgonzola, crumbled*
*Several dashes of Tabasco sauce*
*1 pound fettuccine*
*1½ teaspoons grated fresh lemon rind*
*12 large basil leaves, cut into thin strips*
*6 large mint leaves, cut into thin strips*
*3 ears of white corn, kernels cut from cob and*
*scraped (about 1½ to 1¾ cups)*
*8 thick slices bacon, fried crisp and chopped*

Wilt the onion in the olive oil in a medium skillet over medium heat without browning, stirring, about 5 minutes. Add the salt and evaporated milk, and heat. Add the cheese and Tabasco, and continue to cook over medium-low heat, stirring, until melted and thickened. Remove from heat.

Put the pasta on to cook in salted water. When the fettuccine is almost done, reheat the sauce, adding all other ingredients except the bacon, stirring. Toss the drained pasta with about ½ cup of the sauce and divide among 8 warmed bowls. Top each serving with more sauce (use it all) and sprinkle with bacon.

*Serves 8*

# ROASTED CORN SALSA

◆

Roasting corn can give it a good nutty flavor, but if you don't have the time or inclination, make this with steamed corn.

*1¾ cups fresh corn kernels*
*¾ cup chopped yellow or red onion*
*2 tablespoons minced jalapeño pepper*
*3 tablespoons minced cilantro*
*1¾ cups chopped tomatoes*
*¾ cup chopped sweet red pepper*
*1 tablespoon each fresh lemon, orange, and*
*    lime juice*
*¼ teaspoon salt*
*Pinch of black pepper*
*½ teaspoon soy sauce*

Place a heavy skillet over high heat. When it's very hot, add the corn. Toss constantly until roasted, about 8 minutes. Toss the corn with all the other ingredients. Serve at room temperature, adding more soy sauce if necessary.

*Makes 4 generous cups*

# PEPPERS STUFFED WITH CORN

————◆————

You can use green peppers for this, but I like the way red or yellow ones look. And they *are* slightly sweeter in taste. Either way, choose peppers that will stand easily.

> **6 medium red or yellow bell peppers**
> **2 tablespoons unsalted butter**
> **6 tablespoons minced celery**
> **6 tablespoons minced onion**
> **2 cups fresh corn kernels (scrape the cobs)**
> **1½ cups peeled, seeded, and chopped tomatoes**
> **1½ teaspoons salt (or to taste)**
> **Pinch of black pepper**
> **1 cup soft bread crumbs**
> **2 eggs, lightly beaten (or egg substitute)**
> **1 cup shredded Emmentaler cheese**

Preheat the oven to 350 degrees.

Slice off the stem ends of the peppers and remove the seeds and membranes. Place in a pot of boiling water and cook for about 5 minutes to soften. Drain and set aside.

Meanwhile, melt the butter in a medium skillet over medium heat and cook the celery and onion until wilted, about 5 minutes. Place in a bowl and add the corn, tomatoes, salt, and pepper and toss. Toss in the bread crumbs and then stir in the eggs. Stuff the peppers, mounding with the stuffing. Place in a pan with about ½ inch of hot water, top with the cheese, and cover with oiled foil (the underside). Bake for 50 minutes, uncover, and bake for another 10 minutes to brown.

*Serves 6*

OVERLEAF: *Peppers Stuffed with Corn.*

# CORN RELISH

—◆—

This is another of our family recipes. My Aunt Freddie used to make it every year.

> *¼ cup salt*
> *2½ cups sugar*
> *1 1½-ounce can dry mustard*
> *1 tablespoon turmeric*
> *2 quarts distilled white vinegar*
> *20 ears of corn, kernels cut and scraped from the cobs*
> *1 medium cabbage, sliced*
> *1½ cups chopped green bell peppers*
> *1½ cups chopped red bell peppers*
> *6 large onions, chopped*
> *1 4-ounce jar pimiento, drained and chopped*
> *4 hot red peppers, seeded and chopped*
> *6 to 8 celery ribs, chopped*

In a large pot, combine the salt, sugar, dry mustard, turmeric, and vinegar. Bring to a boil and add all other ingredients. Reduce heat and simmer for 45 minutes.

Spoon the relish into hot sterilized pint jars and fill with liquid, leaving about ¼ inch of head space. Seal. Process for 15 minutes in a boiling water bath.

*Makes 10 pints*

# SAVORY CORN PIE WITH A CHEESE CRUST

Serve this as a main course with a salad, as a side dish for a larger meal—say, with grilled meats or sausages—or as a first course.

### PASTRY

**2 cups flour**
**Pinch of salt**
**½ cup (1 stick) unsalted butter, cut into bits and frozen**
**¼ cup solid vegetable shortening, cut into bits and frozen**
**2 cups shredded cheddar cheese**
**¼ cup ice water**

### FILLING

**4 eggs (or egg substitute)**
**1½ cups half-and-half or evaporated skim milk**
**½ teaspoon salt**
**¼ teaspoon black pepper**
**4 cups fresh corn kernels**
**6 thick slices bacon, cut into ¼-inch strips, fried until crisp and drained**

*Make the pastry:* Toss the flour and salt together in a large bowl. Cut in the butter, shortening, and cheese with 2 knives or a pastry blender until the mixture resembles coarse meal. Stir in the water, mixing well but quickly. Divide in half and form into 2 balls. Flatten each slightly between sheets of waxed paper and chill for 30 minutes.

Preheat the oven to 400 degrees.

Roll out the dough between sheets of waxed paper and line 2 8-inch pie pans. Line crusts with foil and weight down with dried peas or pie weights. Bake for 20 minutes. Remove foil and bake another 10 minutes, until firm. Set aside.

Reduce oven to 350 degrees.

*Make the filling:* Combine all the ingredients except bacon. Process 2 cups of the mixture in a food processor until smooth. Then return the puree to the original mixture and stir it in. Divide the bacon equally between the two partially baked shells. Pour in the corn filling and bake until puffy and set, about 40 to 45 minutes.

*Serves 8 to 12*

OVERLEAF: *Savory Corn Pie with a Cheese Crust.*

# CORN AND SALMON CROQUETTES

——◆——

I've used the minimum of filler with these so they are very tender. They are easy to make and cook, but care should be taken when frying them. When they first start to brown, nudge them slightly to keep them from sticking, then allow them to brown a bit before moving them around and turning them over.

> *1 generous cup fresh corn kernels*
> *1 generous cup skinned, boned, and coarsely*
>    *chopped fresh salmon*
> *3 tablespoons unsalted butter*
> *½ cup minced shallots*
> *¾ cup minced celery*
> *1½ cups soft bread crumbs*
> *2 eggs, lightly beaten*
> *1½ teaspoons salt*
> *Scant ½ teaspoon black pepper*
> *1 tablespoon Dijon mustard*
> *1 tablespoon Worcestershire sauce*
> *Flour*
> *3 tablespoons vegetable oil*

Put the corn into a food processor and pulse a few times. Place corn and salmon in a medium mixing bowl and set aside. Melt 1 tablespoon of the butter in a small skillet and add shallots and celery. Sauté over medium heat until wilted, about 5 minutes. Add to the corn and salmon and toss. Mix in the bread crumbs and enough egg to make a moist mixture. Add the salt, pepper, mustard, and Worcestershire.

Divide the mixture into 6 or 12 portions and form into cylinders. Roll lightly in flour to coat, dusting off excess.

Heat the remainder of the butter and the vegetable oil in a skillet over high heat. When hot, add the croquettes. Turn heat back slightly and fry until golden, about 1 to 1½ minutes, depending on the size. Turn carefully with 2 spatulas and fry other side until golden. Reduce heat slightly and continue to cook until done but not dry, 1½ to 2 additional minutes per side. Turn again if necessary.

*Serves 6*

# CORN AND COCONUT ICE CREAM

———◆———

Now here's a nice surprise. The recipe is Thai in inspiration, and was given to me by Terrell Vermont.

> *2 14-ounce cans unsweetened coconut milk*
> *½ cup sugar*
> *1 cup fresh corn kernels (scrape the cob)*
> *½ cup fresh shredded coconut*
> *½ cup crushed salted peanuts*

Combine the coconut milk and sugar and stir to dissolve the sugar. Add the corn and coconut. Mix well and pour into a metal bowl or tray. Place in the freezer. When almost frozen, stir with a wooden spoon. When really firm, beat it with a wooden spoon.

You can also do this in a commercial ice cream freezer, following the manufacturer's directions.

Sprinkle each serving with the crushed salted peanuts.
*Serves 6 to 8*

# POPCORN BALLS

◆

Another family recipe. If you don't want to go to the trouble of making these into balls, just stir the corn with the syrup until set and serve in a bowl.

*1 cup sugar*
*1 tablespoon distilled white vinegar*
*½ cup water*
*2 tablespoons molasses*
*1 tablespoon unsalted butter*
*½ teaspoon salt*
*6 to 8 cups popped corn*

Put the sugar, vinegar, and water in a large saucepan and bring to a boil over moderate heat. Boil for 5 minutes.

Add the molasses, butter, and salt and cook until a few drops drizzled into a cup of cold water become hard brittle. Remove from heat and stir in the popcorn.

Butter your hands and slip them into baggies. Working quickly, shape mixture into balls, squeezing tightly. When cool, wrap the balls in waxed paper. Store in an airtight container.

*Makes 6 to 8 large, or 15 small balls*

## CORN ON THE COB

*Honestly, is there anyone out there who doesn't think corn on the cob is one of the best things about summer?*

## STEAMED CORN ON THE COB

This method of cooking corn is the best I've ever encountered. It eliminates that problem of keeping corn warm once it's been cooked without overcooking. Here's how you do it. Use a steamer and arrange the ears standing on the stalk ends. Cover tightly and bring the water to a boil over high heat. When the water begins to steam and the lid starts to jump around, time it for 1 minute and then turn off the heat. (If you're using an electric stove, remove the steamer from the coil.) Allow corn to continue cooking by retained heat for 10 minutes more, covered (or a little longer if the corn is not young and fresh) before serving. It can stay like this for up to an hour.

# BARBECUED CORN ON THE COB

◆

Barbecued corn on the cob is a specialty of Trey Wilson, chef-owner of Grandville Cafe in Charleston, South Carolina.

> *1 cup cider vinegar*
> *2 garlic cloves, minced*
> *½ cup Jack Daniel's bourbon*
> *2 tablespoons chili powder*
> *2 tablespoons ground cumin*
> *Pinch of cayenne pepper*
> *1 medium red onion, diced*
> *2 14-ounce bottles ketchup*
> *1½ teaspoons ballpark mustard*

Combine all ingredients except the ketchup, mustard, and corn in a small saucepan. Bring to a boil, stirring, then reduce heat to a simmer and cook for 10 minutes. Stir in the ketchup and mustard off the heat. Let cool, then refrigerate.

Now husk your corn, clean it, and roast it over coals. While it's still hot, brush it all around with the sauce.

## ORN CAKES

*With fresh preserves or syrup, or sprinkled with powdered sugar and topped with poached fruit, the sweet corn cakes here are a delicious breakfast treat. Fill the savory cakes as you would a crepe and top them with one of the sauces from pages 76 to 79.*

## SWEET CORN CAKES

*½ cup flour*
*½ cup yellow cornmeal*
*1 teaspoon baking powder*
*1 tablespoon sugar*
*1 egg, lightly beaten*
*1 cup Creamed Corn (page 28), or canned*
*2 tablespoons vegetable oil*
*About ½ cup milk*

Sift the dry ingredients into a bowl. Mix the egg, corn, and oil in another bowl. Combine the 2 mixtures and then add enough milk to make a thin batter.

Heat a griddle, grease it, and ladle out about ¼ cup of batter for each cake. Cook until the bubbles on top burst, taking a peek from time to time to make sure the bottom isn't getting too dark. Turn and cook until golden on the other side.

*Makes 10 to 12 cakes*

# SAVORY CORN CAKES

—◆—

*¾ cup flour*
*¼ cup yellow cornmeal*
*½ teaspoon baking powder*
*¼ teaspoon salt*
*¼ teaspoon paprika*
*1 cup Creamed Corn (page 28), or canned*
*1 egg, lightly beaten*
*½ cup milk*
*1 tablespoon canola oil*
*1 large ear of corn, kernels cut and scraped*
    *from cob*
*2 tablespoons minced white onion*

Sift the dry ingredients into a bowl. Mix the creamed corn, egg,
milk, and oil and stir into the dry ingredients. Do not overmix.
Cover and allow to rest for an hour or so before cooking.

Heat a griddle and grease it. Stir the corn kernels and onion
into the batter and ladle out a scant ¼ cup for each cake. Cook
until the bubbles on top burst, taking a peek from time to time
to make sure the bottom isn't getting too dark. Turn and cook
until the other side is golden.

*Makes about 24 small cakes*

**RITTERS**

*I'm afraid fritters have fallen out of favor these days, probably because they are deep-fried. But fritters, like onion rings, can be a treat once in a while.*

*The trick with fritters is to have the batter the correct consistency—just thick enough so you have to use a second spoon to urge it off the spoon into the hot oil. Make fritters comparatively small. If they are too large they will not cook all the way through without almost burning on the outside.*

## PLAIN FRITTERS

**1 cup white cornmeal**
**⅓ cup flour**
**2 teaspoons baking powder**
**¾ teaspoon salt**
**2 eggs, lightly beaten**
**1 cup Creamed Corn (page 28), or canned**
**4 to 6 tablespoons milk**
**2 tablespoons minced onion**
**Oil for frying**

Sift the dry ingredients into a mixing bowl. Combine the eggs and corn in another bowl, and mix lightly with the dry ingredients. Add the milk a few tablespoons at a time, until the correct consistency is achieved. Stir in the onion.

Heat oil in the deep-fryer to about 365 degrees. Drop batter by the tablespoonful into hot oil and cook until golden, several minutes. Drain on paper towels.

*Makes about 24 fritters*

# CORN FRITTERS WITH HAM

———◆———

*1½ cups flour*
*2 teaspoons baking powder*
*1 teaspoon salt*
*2 tablespoons unsalted butter, melted*
*2 eggs, lightly beaten*
*About 6 tablespoons milk*
*⅓ cup finely chopped cooked ham*
*1 cup fresh corn kernels*
*Oil for frying*

Mix the dry ingredients in a bowl. Make a well in the center and pour in the butter and eggs. Blend well, and add a few tablespoons of milk. Mix well; the dough should be smooth but not runny, and you should be just able to push it from the spoon with a second spoon. Keep adding milk and mixing until you reach the right consistency. Stir in ham and corn.

Heat oil in the deep-fryer to about 365 degrees. Drop batter by generous tablespoonfuls into hot oil. Cook, turning gently, until dark golden but not burned—several minutes. Test first fritter for doneness before going on, as they can be deceptive, looking done on the outside while still raw in the middle. Drain on paper towels.

*Makes about 24 fritters*

OPPOSITE: *Corn Fritters with Ham.*

OVERLEAF: *Corn and Green Onion Fritters (see page 64).*

# CORN AND GREEN ONION FRITTERS

———◆———

This recipe is from Thai food authority and writer Terrell Vermont. They are crispy and are best eaten just out of the oil, so don't dawdle. Fish sauce, also called *nuoc nam,* is available in many Oriental markets.

> *1 cup rice flour*
> *¾ cup water*
> *1 egg white, beaten lightly with a fork*
> *2 teaspoons fish sauce*
> *1 tablespoon minced cilantro (fresh coriander),*
> *    with stalk*
> *Pinch of curry powder*
> *1 teaspoon freshly ground black pepper*
> *1½ cups fresh corn kernels (scrape the cob)*
> *3 large green onions, with some green,*
> *    coarsely chopped*
> *Vegetable oil for frying*

Mix the flour, water, egg white, and fish sauce in a bowl. Stir until smooth. Stir in the cilantro, curry powder, and pepper, then fold in the corn and green onions.

Heat about ¼ inch of vegetable oil in a large skillet over medium heat until hot, but not smoking. Scoop up batter in ¼-cup measures and add to the oil, cooking 4 or 5 fritters at a time. Cook until lightly golden on the bottom, about 2 to 3 minutes, then turn and cook until golden on the other side. Drain on paper towels.

*Makes about 18 fritters*

## SOUPS

*Corn is a terrific main ingredient in soups and it holds very well. The next time you make gazpacho, add corn to it.*

## CORN CHOWDER

**3 thick slices bacon, cut into ¼-inch strips**
**1 cup coarsely chopped onion**
**4 cups peeled and cubed potatoes**
**2 cups water**
**1 cup crushed oyster crackers**
**½ cup milk**
**2 cups fresh corn kernels (scrape the cobs)**
**1½ teaspoons salt (or to taste)**
**3 dashes Tabasco sauce**
**½ teaspoon black pepper (or to taste)**
**1 cup chicken stock**

Fry the bacon in a large saucepan. Drain. Pour out all but 2 tablespoons of the fat. Add the onion and sauté until lightly browned, about 5 minutes. Add the potatoes and water. Cook over lowered heat until potatoes are tender, about 10 minutes.

Combine the oyster crackers and milk in a small bowl and allow to sit for a few minutes. Stir into the chowder along with the corn, the reserved bacon, salt, Tabasco, pepper, and stock. Simmer over very low heat for another 10 minutes.

*Serves 4 to 6*

OVERLEAF: *Corn Chowder.*

# CORN COB SOUP

———◆———

2 pounds smoked pork neck, cut into several
   pieces (or 1½ pounds smoked shin or
   smoked ham hocks)
3 quarts water (or unsalted chicken stock)
4 large celery ribs, broken into large pieces
1 large bay leaf
2 large carrots, washed and chopped into large
   pieces
6 large sprigs of parsley
12 large ears of corn, kernels cut off and milk
   scraped out, with 6 scraped cobs reserved
2 tablespoons canola oil
2 tablespoons flour
1 cup coarsely chopped green onions with some
   green
½ cup coarsely chopped shallots
1 large red bell pepper, seeded and coarsely
   chopped
1 large garlic clove, minced
2 pounds ripe tomatoes, peeled, seeded, and
   cut into large chunks
1½ teaspoons salt (or to taste)
½ teaspoon white pepper (or to taste)
1 teaspoon paprika

Cover the neck pieces with the water in a large pot. Add the
celery, bay leaf, carrots, and parsley. Break the reserved 6 corn
cobs in half and add them to the pot. Bring to a simmer and
continue to cook very slowly for 2 hours, skimming as needed.

Pour the mixture through a strainer, discarding all the solids. Carefully skim off all fat from the stock and set stock aside.

Heat the oil in a deep pot over medium-high heat. Add the flour and stir until golden. Scrape the roux from the bottom of the pan with a spatula to keep it from getting too brown. Add the green onions, shallots, and red bell pepper. Sauté until vegetables are wilted, about 5 minutes.

Measure out 8 cups of the corn cob stock (add chicken stock if you don't have quite enough of the corn cob) and pour it into the pot. Stir thoroughly to dissolve the roux. Add garlic and tomatoes, and simmer 30 minutes, skimming occasionally.

Pour through a strainer to catch the solids. Puree the solids in a food processor and return to the pot with the stock. Stir in the corn, salt, pepper, and paprika. Simmer over low heat just long enough to cook the corn, about 5 minutes.

*Serves 8*

# CORN AND SMOKED SALMON CHOWDER

◆

*3 tablespoons unsalted butter*
*½ to ⅔ cup finely chopped onion*
*½ to ⅔ cup finely chopped celery*
*½ to ⅔ cup finely chopped red bell pepper*
*2 tablespoons flour*
*3 cups chicken stock*
*2 cups low-fat milk*
*½ teaspoon salt*
*Black pepper to taste*
*2 cups canned or frozen whole kernel corn,*
*drained*
*4 ounces smoked salmon, chopped into pea-*
*size pieces*
*Chopped parsley, dill, or chervil (optional)*

Melt the butter in a large saucepan. Sauté the onion, celery, and red bell pepper over medium heat until wilted and onion is just beginning to brown, about 8 to 10 minutes. Stir in the flour and cook, stirring constantly, for another minute or two. Add the chicken stock and cook for 2 or 3 minutes, stirring. Add the milk and turn heat back to a simmer. Cook for 3 to 4 minutes, stirring occasionally. Add salt, pepper, and corn. Bring back to a simmer and turn off heat. Stir in salmon. Serve immediately, topped with a sprinkling of chopped parsley, dill, or chervil.

If you prefer a thinner soup, use more chicken stock or milk.
*Serves 6*

# CORN AND GREEN CHILI CHOWDER

———◆———

This recipe comes from John Schmidt, chef/owner of the Boonville Hotel, in Boonville, north of San Francisco.

> *¼ cup olive oil or unsalted butter*
> *1 large yellow or white onion, chopped*
> *2 to 3 garlic cloves, chopped*
> *1 yellow bell pepper, seeded and chopped*
> *2 to 3 new potatoes, unpeeled and sliced*
> *4 cups light chicken stock, boiling*
> *½ teaspoon cumin*
> *Salt to taste*
> *3 cups sweet corn kernels*
> *1 8-ounce can green chilis, drained*
> *1 jalapeño pepper, seeded and chopped*
> *¼ cup coarsely chopped cilantro*
> *Black pepper to taste*
> *Sour cream for garnish*

Place 2 tablespoons olive oil in a heavy pot over medium heat and sauté the onion, garlic, yellow pepper, and potatoes until onion is wilted, about 5 minutes. Add boiling stock, cumin, and salt to taste. Continue to cook until potatoes are soft.

Meanwhile, place 2 tablespoons olive oil in a large sauté pan and sauté the corn, chilis, jalapeño, and cilantro until just heated through. Add salt to taste and mix with the stock.

Puree the mixture into a food processor in batches. Pour through a sieve to remove corn kernel skins. Adjust seasoning with pepper and more salt if necessary.

Serve either hot or cold, with a dab of sour cream.

*Serves 6*

# "CREAMED" FRESH CORN SOUP

———◆———

This tasty soup is creamy but contains no cream or milk. It's also extremely easy to prepare. You'll be pleased.

> *2 tablespoons unsalted butter*
> *2 cups thinly sliced leeks, white only*
> *1 cup thinly sliced shallots*
> *6 cups rich chicken stock*
> *3 cups fresh yellow corn kernels (scrape the cobs)*
> *1½ teaspoons salt (or to taste)*
> *½ teaspoon white pepper*
> *Crème fraîche or plain yogurt (optional)*
> *Paprika, herbs (optional)*

Melt the butter in a heavy pot with a tight-fitting lid. Add the leeks and shallots, toss to coat in butter, then place a sheet of waxed paper over the pot before putting on lid. Sweat the vegetables, stirring several times, over very low heat until wilted but not browned, about 15 minutes. Stir in the stock and bring quickly to a boil over high heat, then turn back to simmer. Simmer 15 minutes before adding the corn. When the mixture returns to a simmer, cook another 5 minutes. Puree in a food processor or blender, then strain the soup. Add salt and pepper to taste. Serve warm or chilled with a swirl of crème fraîche or yogurt on top, sprinkled with a little paprika and a sprig of herb if you like.

*Serves 8*

*When corn, particularly white corn, is young and very fresh, it can be used uncooked in tossed salads. Especially salads like the Corn, Butter Bean, and Potato Salad.*

## CORN, BUTTER BEAN, AND POTATO SALAD

*3 medium waxy potatoes, cooked, peeled, and cubed*
*1 15-ounce can white butter beans or white lima beans, drained and rinsed lightly*
*3 ears of fresh young corn, kernels cut and scraped from the cobs*
*⅓ cup olive oil*
*1½ tablespoons lemon juice*
*¼ cup mayonnaise*
*½ teaspoon sugar*
*Salt and black pepper to taste*
*2 tablespoons chopped chives*

Toss together the potatoes, beans, and corn. Set aside.

Whisk together the olive oil, lemon juice, mayonnaise, sugar, salt, and pepper. Fold into the potato mixture. This recipe makes enough dressing to just coat the salad ingredients. If you like your salad with lots of dressing, increase the amounts by half.

Sprinkle salad with chives and mix. Refrigerate for 1 hour, covered, before serving.

*Serves 6 to 8*

# CORN AND SHRIMP SALAD

———◆———

36 medium to large shrimp
6 cups water
1 package shrimp or crab boil
1½ cups fresh corn kernels (scrape the cobs)

### DRESSING

1 egg yolk
¾ cup olive oil
¾ cup peanut oil
¾ cup red wine vinegar
3 tablespoons Dijon mustard
3 tablespoons minced chives or red onion
3 tablespoons minced fresh parsley
1 tablespoon minced shallot

Peel and devein shrimp. Place the water and shrimp boil in a medium saucepan and bring to a boil. Add the shrimp, boil 1 minute, turn off heat, and allow shrimp to cool in the liquid.

Steam the corn kernels for 2 minutes and set aside in the refrigerator.

Whisk together the egg yolk, oils, vinegar, and mustard. Stir in the chives, parsley, and shallot.

Drain the shrimp and place in a serving bowl. Pour the dressing over all, cover, and refrigerate for 2 hours. When ready to serve, stir the corn in with the shrimp. Use a slotted spoon to serve this.

*Serves 6*

*A number of the dishes in this book may be enhanced by a sauce, especially if they are to be served as a first course. Here are a few possibilities.*

## HERB SAUCE

> **1 tablespoon unsalted butter**
> **1 tablespoon plus 2 teaspoons minced shallot**
> **1 heaping teaspoon minced garlic**
> **1 heaping teaspoon minced fresh rosemary**
> **1 tablespoon flour**
> **1¼ cups milk, warmed**
> **½ teaspoon salt (or to taste)**
> **Pinch of white pepper**
> **Pinch of cayenne or several dashes of Tabasco sauce**
> **1 teaspoon Worcestershire sauce**
> **2 tablespoons minced fresh chives**
> **1 tablespoon minced fresh parsley**

Melt the butter in a small saucepan. Sauté the shallot, garlic, and rosemary over medium heat until wilted, about 5 minutes. Stir in the flour and cook for a minute or two. Whisk in milk slowly. Cook over medium-low heat, stirring all the while, until slightly thickened, about 5 minutes more. Off the heat, stir in other ingredients. Serve warm.

*Makes about 1½ cups*

# FRESH TOMATO SAUCE

### ◆

*2 cups peeled, seeded, and coarsely chopped*
  *tomatoes*
*2 tablespoons balsamic vinegar*
*1 teaspoon salt*
*½ teaspoon white pepper*
*1 tablespoon minced fresh dill*

Place all ingredients in a blender or food processor and process just long enough to blend.

*Makes about 1½ cups*


# CUCUMBER SAUCE

### ◆

*1 large English cucumber, peeled, seeded, and*
  *coarsely chopped*
*2 tablespoons tarragon vinegar*
*1 tablespoon canola oil*
*½ cup chicken stock*
*2 tablespoons minced red onion*
*1 tablespoon chopped fresh parsley*
*1 teaspoon salt*
*¼ teaspoon white pepper*

Puree the cucumber, vinegar, oil, and stock in a food processor. Transfer to a bowl and whisk in the other ingredients.

*Makes about 1½ cups*

# WHITE CHEDDAR AND PIMIENTO SAUCE

*1 tablespoon unsalted butter*
*2 tablespoons minced shallot*
*1 tablespoon flour*
*1 cup milk*
*1 cup shredded white cheddar cheese*
*¼ teaspoon salt*
*Pinch of white pepper*
*¼ teaspoon paprika*
*2 dashes Tabasco sauce*
*2 tablespoons chopped pimiento*

Melt the butter in a small saucepan over medium heat. Add the shallot and cook until wilted, about 5 minutes. Sprinkle with the flour and continue cooking, stirring, for a minute or two.

Stir in the milk and continue cooking and stirring slowly until slightly thickened, about 4 or 5 minutes. Remove from the heat and sprinkle in the cheese. Whisk until cheese is melted. Stir in the remaining ingredients. Serve warm.

*Makes about 1½ cups*

## CORN AND RICE

———◆———

Here's a dish I grew up with. I'm not going to give you a recipe, just a method, and the proportions are completely subjective. I suspect this was a way to use leftover rice in our kitchen.

Cook rice in good rich chicken stock. Meanwhile, cut kernels from the cob and cook them in a skillet with just a little milk, cream, or half-and-half until tender. If the corn is fresh and young this won't take but a few minutes. Season with salt and pepper to taste (and a little sugar, if you like). Toss with the rice, pour browned butter over it all, and toss it again. Delicious!